Unlikely Trees

Michael D. Jones

Grey Wolfe Publishing, LLC
PO Box 1088
Birmingham, Michigan 48009
www.GreyWolfePublishing.com

© 2014 Michael D. Jones
Published by Grey Wolfe Publishing, LLC
www.GreyWolfePublishing.com
All Rights Reserved

FIRST EDITION ISBN: 978-1628280258
SECOND EDITION ISBN: 978-1628281552
Library of Congress Control Number: 2014934775

Grey Wolfe Publishing LLC
Ní bóna na coróin

Praise For
Unlikely Trees

"This is an admirable collection, for its range and for its humility, from wonderfully rendered translations, to fixed-form poems, to its casually powerful memory narratives and freer verse. And "collection" is the proper term, here, since the final sense one gets from this carefully made variety is one of gathering, gathering God and family and nature into a set of reflections that deliver the breadth of one life into a complete impression. *So what passes is what is, forever / transformed from within or not at all*, the last poem claims, and to read this volume is to share in that transformation, to read work that merges what is within us to what we are without."

-Edward Haworth Hoeppner, PhD

"I haven't read poetry in probably twenty years. These poems engaged me, and I enjoyed reading and reflecting on them. They are accessible and relevant, and painted pictures that brought my own values and experiences to bear."

-John O'Hara, JD LLM

"These poems will move you by evoking how things are. Some of the poems in this diverse collection are lofty. Others are earthy. They can be difficult, easy, lighthearted, sober, fun. They share beauty by speaking the truth."

-Joseph Laporte, PhD

Praise For
Unlikely Trees

"This is an admirable collection, for its range and for its humility, from wonderfully rendered translations, to fixed-form poems, to its casually powerful memory narratives and freer verse. And "collection" is the proper term, here, since the final sense one gets from this carefully made variety is one of gathering, gathering God and family and nature into a set of reflections that deliver the breadth of one life into a complete impression. *So what passes is what is, forever / transformed from within or not at all*, the last poem claims, and to read this volume is to share in that transformation, to read work that merges what is within us to what we are without."

-Edward Haworth Hoeppner, PhD

"I haven't read poetry in probably twenty years. These poems engaged me, and I enjoyed reading and reflecting on them. They are accessible and relevant, and painted pictures that brought my own values and experiences to bear."

-John O'Hara, JD LLM

"These poems will move you by evoking how things are. Some of the poems in this diverse collection are lofty. Others are earthy. They can be difficult, easy, lighthearted, sober, fun. They share beauty by speaking the truth."

-Joseph Laporte, PhD

Unlikely Trees

Michael D. Jones

Dedication

For my children, who carry me into the new world:

Colleen, Kathryn, Meghan, and Devin.

Acknowledgements

Many thanks to my family for their considered opinions of these works which are first displayed on the side of our refrigerator.

Also, to my community of support that has so generously shared their artworks herein.

- Cover Art, Harbor Springs Landscape, is used with permission of the artist Pierre Bittar http://www.pierrebittar.com/

- "Angel" is used with permission of the artist, Kathleen Chisolm McInerny   http://timothysglove.com/

- "Rainey River Otters" and "O'Connell" are used with permission of the photographer, Christopher Chagnon

- "Anniversary Dinner" and Author Profile pictures are used with permission of the photographer, Kathryn Jones.

- "Bridge Path", "Cityscape", "Riverscape", and "East Chanel Lighthouse" are used with permission of the photographer, Michelle Gray.

- Many thanks to the editors of the following publications, in which early versions of these poems first appeared:
  - *Pudding Magazine:* "Sanctuary Glass"
  - *Legends: Autumn 2013:* "Unlikely Trees" and "Morning Bus Ride"

CONTENTS

II.   UNLIKELY TREES

III.   AFTERWORD

Translated Selected Verse from

Virgil's Aeneid*

*From the 1675 Latin interpretation of Carolus Ruaeus, S.J. (Maronis, Publius Virgilis. *P. VIRGILII MARONIS OPERA, interpretatione et notis illustravit Carolus Ruaeus Soc. Jesu. Jussu Christianissimi Regis, ad usum serenissimu delphini. Secunda editio.* Simonem Benard, Paris, 1682.)

from Virgil's Aeneid
(Aeneidos , Liber VI, 660-689)

Hic manus, ob patriam pugnando vulnera passi: 660
Quique sacerdotes casti, dum vita manebat:
Quique pii vates, & Phoebo digna locuti:
Inventas aut qui vitam excoluere per artes:
Quique sui memores alios fecere merendo:
Omnibus his nivea cinguntur tempora vitta.   665
Quos circumfusos sic est adfata Sibylla,
Musaeum ante onmes: medium nam plurima turba
Hunc habet, atque humeris extantem suspicit altis
Dicite, felices animae, tuque, optime vates;
Quae regio Anchisen, quis habet locus? illius ergo   670
Venimus, & magnos Erebi tranavimus amnes.
Atque huic responsum paucis ita reddidit heros:
Nulli certa domus: lucis habitamus opacis,
Riparumque toros & prata recentia rivis
Incolimus: sed vos, si sert ita corde voluntas,   675
Hoc superate jugum, & facile jam tramite sistam.
Dixit: & ante tulit gressum, camposque nitentes
Desuper ostentat: dehinc summa cacuminal linquunt.
    At pater Anchises penitus convalle virenti
Inclusas aminas, superumque as lumen ituras,   680
Lustrabat studio recolens: omnemque suorum
Forte recensebat numerum, carosque nepotes,
Fataque, fortunasque virum, moresque, manusque.

from Virgil's Aeneid
(Aeneid, Book VI, 660-689)

Here, those warriors that fought and died for country   660
Are celebrated as legend for all eternity
The hallowed dead, Apollo's chosen sons; sung
Into immortality; or, were those favored most by gods
And did their bidding, legendary in their own right
In the afterlife, they too are adorned in robes of white.   665
Like sea-foam they sweep around the Sibyl of Cumea
Great numbers of souls surging, Museaus the foremost
Admirer among the waves, drawn to her supple plea,
Her fertile cry, the cloud sweet god-song of her spirit:
"Who knows beloved Anchises' shade? His renowned   670
Love of Venus brought him across the dark waters."
Recognizing Aeneas now, a few murmured in reply:
"There are no houses here. A sacred grove lies hidden
Beyond the overflowing stream, past the wetlands
He waits; only you can find your hearts' desire there.   675
Master your doubts and embrace the journey ahead.
Listen. You must go. Boldly follow the Sun's path
Heaven sent, your way is clear from the mountain top."
   Meanwhile Anchises' surveyed a green valley full
Of souls crossed over, bathed in heavenly light,   680
And recognized his own tribe, past fathers, sons
And what could be, grandsons' grandsons', and their
Destinies, future homes and families, words and deeds.

Isque ubi tendentum adversum per gramina vidit
Aenean; alacris palmas utrasque tetendit,   685
Effusaeque genis lacrymae, & vox excidit ore:
Venisti tandem, tuaque expectata parenti
Vicit iter durum pietas! datur ora tueri,
Nate, tua, & notas audire & reddere voces!

(Aeneidos , Liber VI, 888-901)

Quae postquam Anchises natum per singula duxit,
Incenditque animum famae venientis amore:
Exin bella viro memorat quae deinde gerenda;   890
Laurentesque docet populous, urbemque Latini,
Et quo quemque modo fugiatque feratque laborum.
    Sunt geminae Somni portae; quarum altera fertur
Cornea, qua veris facilis datur exitus umbris:
Altera, cadenti perfecta nitens elephanto;   895
Sed falsa ad coelum mittunt insomnia manes.
His ubi tum natum Anchises unaque Sibyllam
Prosequitur dictis, portaque emittit eburna.
Ille viam secat ad naves, sociosque revisit.
Tum se ad Caietae recto sert litore portum.   900
Anchora de prora jacitur, stant litore puppes.

Then like a vision coming through the grass he saw
Aeneas running, smiling, his hands outstretched.   685
His cheeks wet with tears, he ran to meet him and cried:
"At last you have come! You have found your Father
You kept the Faith! Your word is blessed with integrity
My son, and now we can talk together freely!"

(Aeneid , Book VI, 888-901)

    After Anchises foretold the succession of his people
Charging his son's spirit with adventures yet to come
He then counseled how Aeneas should go forward   890
With Honor to lead his noble tribe, found their Rome
And appease the gods with their new civilization.
    Two sleep-gates lead out, the second gets you there
The first of horn, sends only vain-wishes and Prayers;
The other brilliant ivory, transports the hard bodies   895
That gods release from this sleepless underworld.
So by these two gates Anchises' son and the Sibyl
Prayed to the gods then left through the ivory one.
Aeneas went back to his ships, reunited with his crew
Then straight to Caietae harbor to make shallow port.   900
Anchors cast from prows, their sterns turned to land.

I.

KALEIDOSCOPE PROJECT

Morning Bus Ride

Sky of my childhood-
tree top, cloud puff, pale moon-
on my way to school.

Kaleidoscope Project

Our young fives program
developing fine motor skills
takes a basket of toilet paper tubes
one for each child
and make kaleidoscopes.
Some add bits of confetti
or plastic beads or small
buttons or broken things
and sealing them between clear
plastic wrap and crinkled
wax paper create
a clouded lens and jumbled
symmetry then learn
not to look directly
into the light.

a camel, a weasel One boy sees
Another girl or a whale.
a hummingbird watches
swim and dog
When in a milky pool.
they will they grow-up
they are have forgotten
they made the tube
and they chose the lens
and they will the shapes and colors
Or, they might have forgotten.
their memory box when visiting
wonder

where
of shiny plastic
their kaleidoscope
Or, changing
roll of toilet paper
remember
directly

the prism
tucked inside
came from.
an empty
they might
not to look
into the light.

"Angel" by Kathleen Chisolm McInerny

Sanctuary Glass

"Every Angel is terrifying." -Rainer Maria Rilke

Girls in sandals. Small birds. Blue panels.
shoeless angels illuminated, arcing
across a sky crowded with open hands,

with large faces, their golden hair streaming
hot-white halos. After thirty years of prayer
one forgets all the praying, chanting, forgets

the words one sings, and becomes the song-
the grain of sand, the flame, those colors
that dance; perfecting ourselves as glass.

Here begins the ineffable terror, not there
in sullied shoes, wrinkled pants, razor stubble,
our wandering eyes and thoughts in church-

the strange comfort, the same story; but here
among beautiful spirits cleansed by the light
of their past. Here I would dissolve entirely

like so many grains of salt into a hot solution,
this pillar of flesh, and riot not to be of glass
ever. Altar-bound. Wing-backed. Forever

beyond the world of Sunday afternoons-
the rustle of leaves, fallen trees, long walks
alone on a rocky path. Alone, and not alone.

Leaves in Winter Light

Early January light;
frost withered leaves twist
in the grass pale as ghosts-
bled-out of their vital
innate green leafy wonder, into
radiant scarlet, orange, and yellow
dried brown in time,
having let go the tree.

Sublime is the point where
our journey becomes
adventure and everything elevates
erratically, dancing like trees
when the winds descend
and branches bounce beneath
Heaven's clear blue dome.

Sublime is the moment we let go
and nothing real is lost.
What was is
and will be forever, although forever
changed by the seasons;
their palpable flow and predictably
leafy cycles, ripe
with the fruit of our lives,
as busily we travel in circles
around a living sun
that guides the seasons,
provides us hope and,
that like us, was born to shine.

"Winter Trees" by Michael D. Jones

Another Tree Poem

My mom would like another tree poem.

It is my fault, I told her that
the polar vortex left the trees
all white on one side and almost two feet
of powder, knee deep, in our woods out back.
She said that sounded lovely, and I should write
another tree poem about the snowy trees.

She has been my mother forever,
or for at least the past fifty-plus years;
and it is my job to fall for her ploys.
Among other things, I promised her
long ago not to give away her age
and to stop counting the laugh-lines
and tear-tracks, the natural profit of love,
like the rings inside of trees.
                              So, she's
fifty-plus-plus and this is not about trees.

Colleen Means Girl

For Colleen

Every name tells a story.

We had never met a Colleen
at school or on the playground
who was not last born, a sport
of Irish name, and happy just to be
here, where you were wanted.

We had never met a Colleen
who was not kind and true
and knowing, whose eyes deepen
with conviction like the blue sea-
sparkle with wonder like the night.

In your case Colleen means girl
we had waited long for; our last
girl who would share the face
of Angels manifest
in the night's dark window.

Lady

She drinks me in, her large nostrils
flaring; wide eyed, ears pricked,
all horse- her majestic chestnut
thick neck, tall back, swept mane
at rest in her stall- eyeing me,
breathing me in- she intuits
my body heat, hormones, heart rate,
prayer life, the poems I write,
whatever horses know by smell;
silent, yet all-a-go, beneath
her twitching skin and swishing tail,
like a Sybil in her dark cave
she wants answers, and tells me so.

She hates the shit and darkness, hates
the horse flies, metal bits, Mondays,
stallions, whatever God did this
to her, blessed her with speed
and a love for jumping gates,
with never enough pasture land
and tall, no jump, safety fences;
gave her nearly a wisp of a girl,
a guardian who mucks her stall
and feeds her apples, carrots,
half flakes of hay, and peppermints.
Slowly Lady puts a lump of sugar
On my tongue; wide eyed, ears pricked.

After the Turkey Hunt

I must confess; I have never hunted Turkey.

I have often thought, watching a rafter of turkeys
cross M-32 in winter, cars stopped both ways,
how turkeys survive at all in the wild.

And, for the first time last year, I saw a turkey
sleeping at dusk in our sugar maple out back
uphill from the pond.
                    It seemed unnatural
all by itself, far from the ground, balanced.

I have seen hawks sway perched atop pine trees
graceful, majestic birds scanning the tall grass
for mice.
          Or herons, their massive wings tucked
on low branches of dead wetland trees, hunting frogs.

And then, at church last fall we played Bingo
for Turkeys
        and Tofurkeys and Tur-duck-hens
(frozen, of course; an "old-bird" hunt of sorts
even some "old-birds" hunt.)
                  And Turkeys hunt.
They forage, forage, forage, forage, forage,
forage, forage, scrabble, scrabble, scrabble,
scrabble, seeds and gravel, seeds and gravel,

wild berries, caterpillars, loose roots, young shoots,
their talons, their sharp beaks, peck and claw,
tear the ground into abundance.
                                        They remind me
of Puritans and Gnostic poets: Taylor
Bradstreet, Longfellow, Poe, Whitman-
                                        Me imperturbe-
they know how to succeed; peaceful, humble,
measured, persistent, social, wild game afoot.

I sometimes wonder how poets survive at all.

About Now

Now is a short bus ride on the longest road north.
Shopping lists are Now,
even though they may take days to create,
as they are always being rewritten.

Now refuses to speak to voice mail,
has an unlisted number, and is often suspected
of moonlighting as a telemarketer.
At the Discotheque, Now fell in love
and danced all night, beneath
the mirrored ball and strobe light.
Or, maybe it was just a dream.

Now implies here everywhere,
making Now a singular paradox.
Now needs no introduction and has no reputation.

Now is the best part of a Now 'n Later candy
as later usually involves the Dentist.
"Don't look now, too late!" is Now's favorite joke.
"Are we there, yet?" is a close second.

Tennis was Now's favorite sport.
While covering a drop shot, Now rushed the net,
twisted an ankle and tore a tendon. It seems that
on cold rainy days Now limps along more slowly.

Now is a farting horse moving sharply
in all directions at once yet never going very far.

Now finds hiccups annoying,
but secretly has a thing for echoes.

In another life, Now would be a Leprechaun.
Now dressed-up as Sherlock Holmes one Halloween,
complete with pipe and pocket watch, and handed out
ice cream treats. The neighbors were not amused.

Take nothing but pictures, leave nothing but footprints
is Now's Ars Persona, which gives rise to the syllogism;
if Now is to Pictures what Dark Matter is to the Universe,
then Bob's your Uncle.

On my way to one last appointment
before leaving town on vacation,
I passed Now hitchhiking- arm extended,
thumb out- which is illegal in most States.
Moved by recognition and regret
I glanced back and broke, but Now was gone.

"Nnaaa, Nnnaaaaa. Oowww, Ooowwwww…"
Now is the first word all babies speak in
the language of Angels announcing their arrival
and sounds like inconsolable sobbing
to those that have forgotten.

Now looks like a wet dog shaking itself dry,
yet tingles like a kiss.

And, that is about it, for Now.

The Farmer, His Wife and the Scarecrow

He in his denim overalls, flannel shirt,
red neckerchief and John Deer cap,
could have been a middle-aged scarecrow-

his beard prickly as straw, his teeth
uneven as corn, eyes like coal bricks,
stuffing gone soggy from the rain,

and rough hands. This he had done
to himself, and she still loved him.
He would say to himself, She loves me

when he was alone, usually at night
after the TV began to snow. She let
him drive to town Sunday mornings

to church, and sat with him in her
perfumed silence and hat. The town
knew what he was, and who she was,

and it was at church one Sunday where
she heard Angels, heard their voices,
heard that television snow was bad,

an empty bed was bad, her husband
was bad in his middle-agedness; that he
was a scarecrow she had made all soggy

and benign; and she was bad for
not being better, for her hat and silence.
The Angels followed her to the farm

in her disbelief. They spoke like bacon
at breakfast, they spoke cicada at dusk,
and when it began to rain they stopped,

washed their hands in the storm pipe,
and went back to the place of Angels;
which is what she told the scarecrow

rotting out in her husband's cornfield,
and what she told her husband when
he found her talking to the scarecrow

in the rain, her perfume all but gone.

"Anniversary Dinner" by Kathryn Jones

Silver Chains

One hundred seasons-
the silver wind in our hair-
our God between us.

Our Beloved

For Kelly and Erik Dahl, 7.19.2003

You are beloved in this world, beneath this vast sky
Which is familiar and immense, clear blue
And cloud grey, unfolding with the seasons,
Obedient to the inclinations of a transrational sun:

Oh, what a Sun! What a marriage! How perfect
The physics, the ride through the heavens together
Distinct and inseparable, husband and wife,
Day and night, heat and light, pine trees and roses.

You are beloved in this world where synergy
Is celebrated, marriage ventures forth a new family
With a joy no less thunderous than the birth of stars. Yes
What brave confluence of choice has brought us here?

Happy the days you were born into this great dance,
Happy the floor you crossed to meet, happy your tea cups.
Greater are we for your union. Greater are you for our love.
Greater each day that lay ahead for this world.

You are beloved in this world, in your Spring
You are sure footed as the gazelle that leaps
Into its day, darting through the tall grasses,
Winding along rocky mountain paths. You risk

Yourselves through love into marriage. Travelers
In purpose, together at days end, beloved in this world
Can you measure the light, the distance of your doing,
Will your footfalls echo like shadows across the mountains?

You are beloved in this world by those of us who
Watch you cross the floor, hear your footsteps:
Neighbors before you, neighbors behind you, next to you
Witnesses today of your love into marriage: family
And friends, our intentions and prayers
A covenant we share with you in this world

Our beloved.

Saturday Mornings

I like to mow the lawn around our house.
Both spring and fall I wait for the grass
to dry enough so it will not clump
when mulched, and also so my shoes
stay dry. You can learn much from chores.

My father preferred to work our gardens
and rake the leaves from their severely edged
grass line each fall enough to work
the leaf blower in concentric circles
and oddly formed a mounded line
snaking through our yard. In spring
and summer he would pluck the weeds
and snap off the dead and dying flowers.

When I mow the lawn, I alternate
patterns, and twice a year start around
the big maple out back unwinding tracks
in circles moving outward and consider
entropy, bits of verse by Yeats
and my father now retired in Florida.

I miss mowing the lawn in the winter.
So I vacuum the house, even hardwood
and tile floors. Both the dog and cat
shed hairs which clump in corners like grass
reminding me of unmulched grass
in carpet, except carpeting likes
to move with the grain, and not across-
while grass delights in patterned change.

Joanne has mixed feelings about winter
house chores, as I tend to rearrange
the furniture when vacuuming based
on whatever carpet lines are working well.
Sometimes the couch ends up at odd
angles, and chairs turned upside down
will rest on table tops all weekend long.
It bothers her when I go off
indulging momentously my love
for her around the house on Saturdays.
We often end up together- unchorelike.

"Riverscape" by Michelle Gray

Tahquamenon

I.

Colleen knows, every name tells a story.
The names of rivers are my favorite.
Go on, think of a rivers' name:
I like Tahquamenon. It sounds

mysterious and exotic as
Hiawatha, French fur trappers,
and the northern tribes that named
and navigated those amber waters;

tannin heavy from cedar swamps
flooded by spring thaws and rains-
the river meanders, rushes, and falls
then pools and glides gently along-

Tahquamenon, and on, and on.
Here is what I like most: the river
bed shifts, banks move, generations
of trout doze behind fresh fallen trees,

late each year the salmon return,
the waters have changed and yet,
as I gaze both up and down stream
recognizing other rivers

I have traveled: the story and name,
reflection and run, remain the same.

II.

What is in a name?

The inherent sound

and inflection of things?

The horse-i-ness

or happiness, the game

or sport

of cultural imperatives?

The associative

relational subtleties

and innate

visceral integrities

of sorts?

Theoretically, I suppose.

Still,

in practice,

qualities persist.

III.

Suppose, in the end, there is only
a great emptying out into *what?*

truth temporal like a salmon spawn
or river run, downstream flow

and upstream swim, all movement,
music and dance, a joyous confluence

we sense beyond our senses:
Tahquamenon of the familiar
fresh waters into the foreknown.

Now, is your story any less
mysterious and exotic as
it fills, changes and empties itself?

And, have you, at last engendered
a rivers' name to claim? Go on.

Hypothesis Concerning Origins of the Self-Evident

Everybody knows a great flood
Nearly washed the earth clean of life
And things were not always
As they appear, and will not be;
And there is more than we can know
Beyond our finger tips and lips
And so we make up stories and gods
Personifying the obscured truth.

The Greek Theogeny at best
Separated us from our better selves
Made us less than we are; but gave
Us Prometheus, Epimethius
And Atlas---
                    everything we need
To crucify the human and divine.

II.

UNLIKELY TREES

Becoming What I Find

Cicadas and fresh cut grass; a hot summer's day-
I could be six again, riding my bike, losing teeth,

bed head hair, swimsuit for underwear on my way.
Today, it is meetings and marketing; bright red ties

pleated slacks, cell phones, day planner, and lunch.
Four kids of my own and it is fashionable to roll

with mismatched socks and no-iron shirts.
                                        Here I am.
Des Moines or Detroit, it really doesn't matter now

the wheel come round, it's curious wobble
reminiscent of first things; spinning tops,

swinging gates, rolling balls, best friends-
Billy, Davey, John John, Jo, Wendy, Becky, Este-

freeze tag, dam sliding, shenanigans and ice cream:
Memories of becoming what I find myself to be.

"Bridge Path" by Michelle Gray

Unlikely Trees

Not just another Midwestern fall weekend.
October sunlight, mellow air, Joanne really big

with child, our first, traveling west on two lane
scenic roads, on our own. Rolling past the Irish

Hills, antique shops, local bars, rest stops, then north
to Ludington, along Lake Michigan, steel blue

and jagged behind autumn's quilted landscape
summer's green burst into unlikely flame, again.

Somehow the fiery trees seem less terrified than we
by abrupt endings and certain bold beginnings.

To get out and walk the low bluff dunes helps. Hike
from the road side "For Sale" sign to the shifting edge

of tree line, past birch and pine, to sugar sand beach–
a small measure of peace: flushed and breathless.

Public House

Friday constitutional at the Pub; A Drink Comes
Before a Story in Gaelic script, peat smoke

Fiddle and drum, plank floors and clay walls, runic
in their desire. "Jamesons whiskey, rocks please, double."

Some stories take longer, the parishes of Detroit
reach back to French garrisons and frontier traders-

today mine takes one double. Turn off your cell phones
loosen your coats, light-up smokes,
                                        I drink deep not fast.

When God speaks I hear only echoes on mountain sides
in valleys bathed in cloud. Often the meaning is lost

or I misunderstand: my hearing is imperfect. So, God
speaks in other ways; like the time my wife, Joanne

on our drive to visit my nephew Jack, told me
about Fat-ass the Cat, then Nina's adoption secret.

Lines 1

Trees at night outside the airplane window
Their boughs heavy with December ice, wave

Goodbye. Detroit fades behind dark clouds.
Faith; everything will be fine, love's sacrifice

Like giving blood then blacking out. Tonight
Devin jets into his future. First stop, Cal Tech

Where baseball and engineering, twin loves
Favor bold beginnings. Everything is fine.

Advent purple, candles in a circle, pray and wait
Half a lifetime, then one day a calling. Be brave.

I learned to ride a bicycle when it was time
And pushed up-hill: Legs pumping, bike weaving

Down I flew not knowing how to turn, wide eyed
The bumpy road and Life's soft promise. It is all fine.

"Rainey River Otters" by Christopher Chagnon

Lines 2

The baby turtle was frantic over the garden hose
By my front door, where new plantings flowered

After I had roto-tilled and fertilized last month.
The loose earth bathed in lamp light looked

The perfect place to dig down and release a clutch
And cover-up, before trekking back to the moonlit

Pond out back.   Baby turtles die all the time trying
To get back home; lawn mowers, hawks, electric lights.

This one I named Michelle. By Labor Day, Shelley
Balanced on her rock, would stretch toward Jo's voice

Take from her hand. When we released Shelley back
Into the pond, she swam to the nearest algae clump

Freely. I'm not saying this is how adoption works;
Only why we, too, follow the singing in the night.

"Cityscape" by Michelle Gray

Lines 3

I.

Knee-wall to ceiling, the office windows are fixed
Giant screens where unspoken dramas play

And I'm on the sidewalk, all street noise and bustle
Theatre of the audience. My reflection

Dark among the fluorescent workers milling
Like tulips, or snowflakes, or white-clad labor

And delivery nurses. The splendor of a window
Slowly opening. Is it so wrong to question

Now that seasons have turned back and the sun
Flashes against the window, cleansing the darkness

My reflection dissolving in pools of light-
What will become of us when nothing remains

For conjecture? No doubts, no fears, no hopes.
Can this be the start? Are you really here at last?

II.

Diaper rash. Skin burned raw from repeated pee.
My tears ran hot and inconsolable as bees

After the harvest. The echo of my cries buzzed
And lulled me to sleep, which is how they got me

Asleep; swaddled in a clean, dry, sleeper. Wrapped
Rosy cheeked in a blanket, the very picture of baby

Easy to love, a little brother for their other back home.
What a blessing. Small hands. Skinny butt. Runt-runt.

Who could know a six week old babes furious need
For love? The cries were piercing, the rash ran all over

And sleep did not last. Peace would be fought for
In this new land, and peace would be made. Secure

Coddled in a mother's arms, close-in on a shoulder
While she vacuumed everything: over, and over.

Lines 4

Early Lenten Friday: breezy, mild. I met
Galen Wickersham mid-stride

On Humphrey Street, half-way up
The sidewalk. My idea to view the vacant

Home in Birmingham for a fussy client
And neighbor Galen looking after the place

Dropped over to chat. Owned his house
Since Sixty-one, when he worked design

For General Motors.   Blue sky, some cloud
The spirit took my tongue, I knew, I said

Someone there in Sixty-two, Uncle Jim.
"Oh, Jim", says Galen, "I drove to South Bend

Interviewed Jim for that job. Still see him."
Funny, that's how I came here, too. Amen.

Lines 5

Fat-ass the Cat is dead. Let us pray for Fat-ass.
Wonderful, marvelous, cat I never met.

Were you a mouser or hunter of the invisible
Threat? I bet you liked to sit around the house.

How many children snuggled, chased, and teased
The life from you, well loved cat. Whiskers or Bob

Could not have done the job, no first-grade teacher
Would snicker and share the prayer for Fat-ass the Cat.

That is how it all began. Little Hanna's aunts cat passed.
Too late, the name let fly. Debate about propriety

And children. Good thing it wasn't abortion. We pray
For those who carry the pain of loss, but who prays

After forty years for the pain of absence, and who
Celebrates timely endings and bold beginnings?

Lines 6

God Bless adoptive parents, their star-struck lives
Church groups, holidays, cocktail parties, work

The soft abundance of clouds and city lights.
They suffer no less the more they are denied

Beyond their will and wishes for their children
Ones to call their own, the want they alone can name

And fill their ears with childhoods sound. To share
Childhood in their covenant, grow together in age.

Red toothbrush, red towel, red cup; my color
Chosen carefully as the names of planets. Michael

"We wanted Douglas, but you cried too much."
Then happiness, laughter, footsteps lightly pounding

Wild fights, broken vases, late nights; the fields
Where parents are forged, where love reigns.

Exiles

I.

Midlife, midstream, mid-stride, road weary, dazed,
descent the unspoken command, I follow the path.

What is there to question? Free-willed, faith-filled
diplomas on the wall, family pictures down the hall-

I've traveled some. Bridge May Be Icy; Slippery Road
Ahead.
        In 1963, God was alive and well in Michigan

and Catholic Social Services brokered my adopted name.
Last night, kids asleep, Joanne and I drank wine and wept

for the darkened path before us raised uncertain ghosts.
They swam in reflections beyond our picture window

behind my chair, and Joanne saw the one she claimed
the child we never had. Family was all I knew

then. We vowed never... Who would not think
the less of us? The shame of knowing better. Ghosts.

II.

Aunt Judy knows it's genetic. That's a first for me.
and, Patrick Sarsfield, age of twelve, sailed from Dublin

for New York. Imagine. The great famine
decimated the country, nearly half died or left-

I have read the histories. Iron men and wooden ships
ex-patriots packed shoulder to shoulder, farm animals

to slaughter, their groaning hulls sailed out of harbor.
Many, unworthy, sank within sight of land. All was lost.

Patrick, Earl of Dispossession, survivor of perilous seas
arrived alone at Ellis Island, and initiated

with misspelled name signed on to an Orphan Train
and headed west into the heartland. At his last stop in Iowa

after others in Pittsburgh, Cleveland, Chi-town, St. Louis
were claimed; a farmer and his wife found their boy.

III.

Ireland sinking in waves behind them, the Wild Geese
could see the promise of France. The Irish Army

upholding treaty, sailed into exile with James to war
for profit in Europe. Iron men in wooden ships

sacrificing their past for the future. A fair bargain,
the Treaty of Limerick, Church bells and hymn books

sang in the peace for Ireland, and Thanks be to God:
Schools, land, equality.
                                          Within a year the treaty broke.

Many prayed for General Sarsfield, his Geese, their
return home victorious, prosperous with King James

warriors laden with horse, cannon, bow and arrow,
double-crossing the channel, liberating their families.

Iron men. Sacrifice. Honor. Mortal wounds.
If... for Ireland. An epitaph in Belgium.

East Channel Lighthouse" by Michelle Gray

Until

Cigars, an antidepressant; household chores help, too.
Suddenly I can't sell snowballs, my drop-eyed dog

won't leave me alone, Devin is looking at out-of-state
schools (Cal Tech, maybe), Jo says her body's done

enough, needs a rest. Even my midlife sports car
durable relic, monument to Big Al (more best friend

than dog) seems dispassionate about the road.
Last night I couldn't sleep- the terrors kept me awake.

My prayers have all been answered with pain not mine.
My self-reliance given way to power beyond me.

From within me, as if struck by lightning, magnetized
paperclips of grief come flying back to me with little

notes: If only; Remember; Meet me; Go West.
I'm keeping off the booze until the love returns.

The Practice of Miracles

Miracles are at least
one part terror; the blood streaming
from the Saint's stone eyes, the blind man's

first look on his beloved, delight of the cripple
healed who walked
until gravity squished cartilage

into tingling numbness. Now live this forever.
Miracles are also then one part ecstasy

which is why we witness
the miraculous around us-
Saints, Angels, and ghosts.

Did you hear anything?

God is speaking. Listen. Miracles
are at least one part
hidden like the rain and the sun
in clouds, revealed both
within and beyond us.

If not, the stone could not weep,
nor the blind see, nor the cripple
delight in the tingling numbness
of traveling far; perhaps all the way
back to Des Moines or Dublin,
or years ahead to Detroit: to see and bleed.

Summer Days

The summer days will never end

the sky will never rest
like waves on Little Traverse Bay

their chop and gleam a geometry
of persistence that (I joke
while lighting my cigar)
is almost unnaturally futile.

Still, the waves claw against the shore
of their own making; exhausted.

It would be vastly different
if it were winter dark.

Instead, I would admire
the brilliant moon, full of otherness

radiant, pressing out into and
through the darkness

on Little Traverse Bay,

                           as I hike

uptown to Pete's smoke shop.

"O'Connell" by Christopher Chagnon

Afterword

Two Gates

You must choose a gate or else
stay where you are, but you are not
at home eating spaghetti, red wine

bottles passed among friends, family
like a chain around the long table
nor are you alone on an island

with just three wishes and a tree
nor are you where you want to be.

There are two gates, always two gates-
one we pass through and the other
we cannot; you cannot pass through

the one, no matter how good it looks
or whatever promise it holds. The gods
or a god (but not God) built the gates.

The gates are not ours, they are bigger
like the mouth of a river emptying
into a river from the sea, backwards

gates we must enter like mighty fish
swim upstream, and find the source.

Or, more likely, the gates are imagined

and what happens next is a matter
of faith, character and knowledge.

So what passes is what is, forever
transformed from within or not at all.

Either way, your Father will be there.

By Kathryn Jones

Michael D. Jones

Unlikely Trees is a collection that explores. It travels on foot, by car, bus, plane, and ship. Yet, it is through people, places, and things which the poems work to discover the better part of our humanity- faithfulness, love, compassion, forgiveness, sacrifice, hope and perseverance. It possesses an image-bearing intensity that often allows for small and common things (like a morning bus ride or a leaf) to become expansive, luminous and transformative; and reduces the seemingly overwhelming to basic elements. Michael Jones poems possess a sensibility that is associative and offer a perspective that indulges in the everyday wondrous and miraculous.

Michael Jones has a Master of Arts degree from Oakland University and a Bachelor of Arts degree from the University of Michigan.

www.ingramcontent.com/pod-product-compliance
Lightning Source LLC
Chambersburg PA
CBHW071839020426
42331CB00007B/1786